AF334010

SONNETS

OF

ESCAPE

AND

DISCOVERY

Written by

Judith Weinshall Liberman

Published by
Judith Liberman
Westwood, MA 02090

4904_1

ISBN Numbers:

Paperback: 978-1-7373924-7-7

Hardcover: 978-1-7373924-6-0

****

This book is dedicated with love to
the memory of my dear husband

ROBERT LIBERMAN

who always supported and
encouraged me.

Judith Weinshall Liberman

****

מִבֶּטֶן

שְׁאוֹל

שִׁוַּעְתִּי

שָׁמַעְתָּ

קוֹלִי

BOOK OF JONAH 2: 2 (Hebrew)

PREFACE

I was ninety-two years old when I wrote the sonnets presented in this book. I did so in 2021, during the COVID-19 pandemic. Writing my sonnets offered me a welcome distraction from the daily tragic news.

This is my tenth book of poems. Before writing the sonnets contained in this book, I had already published nine books of poems: *REFLECTIONS* (with my daughter, Laura Liberman, M.D.) in 2012, *PASSION* in 2013, and seven books of sonnets in 2021. My books of sonnets were: *SONNETS OF LOSS AND TRIUMPH, SONNETS OF PAIN AND FORGIVENESS, SONNETS OF SETBACK AND HOPE, SONNETS OF GRIEF AND PRIDE, SONNETS OF BETRAYAL AND ACCEPTANCE, SONNETS OF POWER AND HONOR* and *SONNETS OF ENVY AND EXILE*. I had also previously published a book titled *ZINA* (2013) about my mother's life and poetry.

I selected the sonnet form to write my recent poems in because of the challenge of that form. The brevity of sonnets compelled me to get to the core of my ideas and to try to express my thoughts clearly and concisely.

The Old Testament story of Jonah plays an important part in the present book. Jonah's attempt to escape God's command, and his discovery that there was no escape, have reverberated with me increasingly through the years.

These sonnets are intended to convey some of the important lessons I have learned during my long life.

Judith Weinshall Liberman

1

I've often wondered why, O Jonah, your
escape from your God seems to ring a bell.
It makes me think of times I did endure
the pain of which I am about to tell.

In fact I do see in your bold escape
a symbol that connects your life to mine.
Across the ages and the old landscape,
there is from you to me a direct line.

I'll try now to explain why I can see
in your escape a symbol of my life,
though my belief in God could never be
as strong as yours was even in times of strife.

What is it in your story that I deem
to be a symbol of my own life's scheme?

2

You'd been a prophet of your God, I know,
for a long time, and faithfully obeyed
whatever your God asked of you, to show
you'd never think of having Him betrayed.

And yet one day when your God called on you
to go to Nineveh and there preach to all
that Ninevites must to your God's word be true
or their whole city would be doomed and fall,

you did not follow what your God had said.
You did not go to Nineveh, but, we're told,
you headed west and not toward east instead,
thus made a move that was indeed quite bold.

Why was it that you suddenly wished to hide
from your own God, who'd always been your guide?

3

Why is it you refused then to obey
your God's command that you now go and preach
in Nineveh, so that save the town He may
if Ninevites followed lessons you would teach?

I know that Nineveh was indeed the foe
of your own nation so you'd not partake
of saving Nineveh, for that would be a blow
to your own nation (thus a big mistake).

Was your flight personal to some extent?
You wished to stay away from any strife.
You knew that Ninevites were violent.
Perhaps you simply feared for your own life.

I wonder if you had the introspection
to put your motives under close inspection.

4

You reached the shore and then you found a port
where boats were loading passengers, I've read.
You quickly boarded so you'd be sure to thwart
your God's command to head inland instead.

Where were you going, Jonah, now to be
far from your God so you could just ignore
His order that you go to Nineveh (and not flee
your God's command perhaps forever more)?

To Tarsus, which was far across the sea,
a place of legends, as I understand.
Apparently you thought Tarsus would be
beyond the reach of your own God's firm hand.

You thought that you could hide in Tarsus, though
you should have known God follows wherever you go.

5

You went to sleep. You trusted that your boat
would reach the port of Tarsus, where you'd debark.
Perhaps you dreamed of a smooth and steady float,
and clear blue skies, a sea that was not dark...

But while you slept your God was busy making
His moves against you, as in a game of Chess:
He brought about a storm that could be breaking
the boat where you were sleeping. What a mess!

The captain and his crew, who were on board,
to save the boat from sinking in the storm
now tossed their precious cargo overboard.
But doing so helped in no shape or form.

How could the boat on which you tried to hide
be saved from your own God before all died?

6

It seems that at long last you were awake.
You realized that something was amiss.
You went on deck and saw what was at stake:
Your boat could sink straight into the abyss!

You knew right off it was your God who had
created the great storm in the vast sea
to punish you, Jonah, for being bad
by trying your own God in fact to flee.

You told all those on board that it was you
who bore responsibility, in fact,
for you had disobeyed, and, in your view,
now God was meting punishment by His act.

There is no doubt that you should be commended:
Your insight and your candor were not suspended.

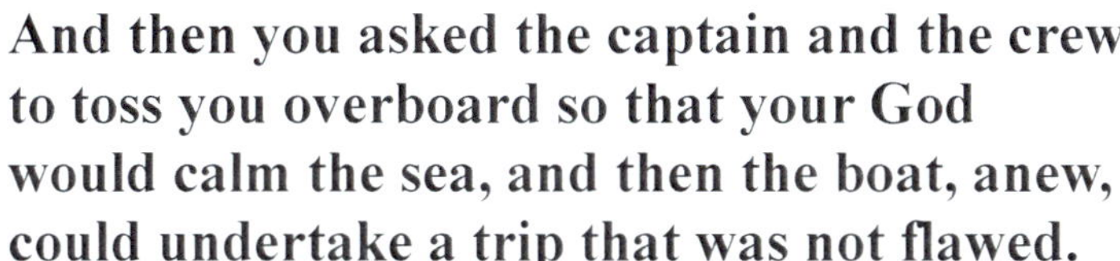

7

And then you asked the captain and the crew
to toss you overboard so that your God
would calm the sea, and then the boat, anew,
could undertake a trip that was not flawed.

The captain and the crew, though, did not feel
you were indeed the cause of the great storm,
but then they cast some lots that did reveal
you'd failed to your God's wishes to conform.

So then they picked you up and promptly tossed
you right into the raging deep dark sea.
Perhaps you thought you were forever lost,
and never would the light of day then see.

Was drowning you what your God had in mind?
Or did your God plan nothing of the kind?

8

In fact for you to drown was not His wish.
He had some other plans in store, for sure.
He went ahead and told a great big fish
to swallow you quite whole so you'd endure.

Now that big fish obeyed your God's command
and swallowed you quite whole, so then, it seems,
you were somewhere you did not understand
and thought you might be having awful dreams.

In that dark place you reached out to your God
and prayed to Him from the belly of the fish.
It seems you did repent, which was not odd
because now to be saved was your true wish.

Was your God moved when He thus heard you pray
to rescue you though you had run away?

9

Three long days in the belly of the fish
thus spent by you in prayer to your God
now moved your God to finally grant your wish
and rescue you (and thereby spare the rod).

God then commanded the big fish to spit
you right onto dry land so you would live.
The fish obeyed your God's command, for it
was clear that in fact your God did forgive.

You then agreed to go to Nineveh after all.
It seems you were now truly a changed man.
Sometimes it takes great pain for one to call
on one's own strength and carry out a plan.

The end of your old tale I will now tell.
It shows that all in fact ended quite well.

10

You then went right to Nineveh, there to preach,
and urged its folk to stop their evil way
but rather treat all people well and reach
up to your God's high standards from that day.

And much to your surprise, without delay
the Ninevites did hear you loud and clear.
They were transformed and followed your God's way
so all could live together without fear.

And so your God spared Nineveh in the end.
Its people had repented, just like you.
Since once your way God did forgiveness send,
It's right that He forgave the Ninevites, too.

How did you feel at last when you were told
your nation's foe would flourish as of old?

11

It's baffling to read that when your God
decided that the Ninevites should be spared,
you felt that His decision was quite flawed
and to voice your disappointment you then dared.

You had regrets that you had been appealing
to Ninevites their old ways to avoid.
I think you were quite swayed by your deep feeling
that your own nation's foe should be destroyed.

Perhaps you did not trust your nation's foe
to follow in God's way forever more,
But your God had forgiven you, and so
He figured sparing Nineveh was in store.

So how does your old story thus outlined
now bring my own life's story to my mind?

12

My God and yours were clearly miles apart:
Mine was not one residing way out there.
My God was living right inside my heart.
He tried to guide me, but I was unaware.

Why was it that to flee my God I tried?
I closed my ears and therefore could not hear
that He was calling me from deep inside
to follow where He'd lead me, far or near.

I do regret I did not hear my God.
I spent so many years just playing roles
that then turned out to be vastly at odds
with my own nature and my life's true goals.

What is the reason that I failed to hear
a voice that should have been so very clear?

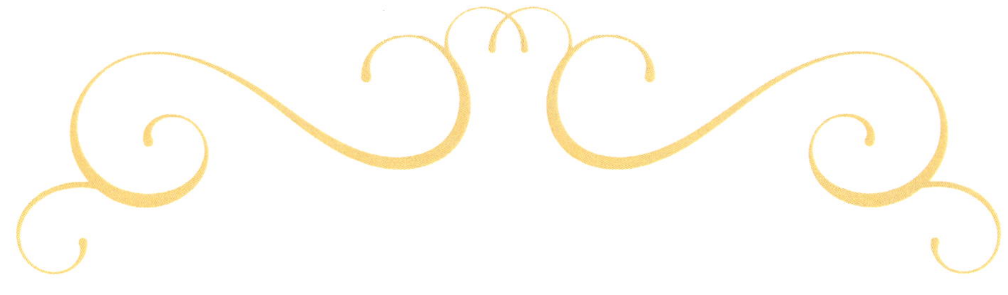

13

It's painful to recall the many ways
I stumbled on my road to self-awareness.
It took long years made up of many days
for me to hear my inner voice, in fairness.

Although I should have known right from the start
I was an artist and would never find,
while spending my time not creating art,
anything resembling peace of mind,

I still spent years in searching far and wide
for the true calling that would bring me peace,
and all that time I did my best and tried
to fill my roles with competence and ease.

So many roles did I then try to fill
on my long road to hearing my God's will!

14

I still recall all those delightful hours
I spent, while still a child, creating things:
like weaving baskets out of leaves and flowers,
and making scarves of bits of colored strings,

using Persian miniatures as models for
some watercolors that were bright and gay,
and African dark wooden mask and more
for doing some line drawings every day.

Perhaps when we are children we reveal
What's in our heart and just what we should do;
We're then in touch with what in fact is real
before the world clouds what for us is true.

To parents everywhere I wish to say:
be sure to watch you little child at play!

15

Although I did do well all those long years
when I attended grammar through high school,
my favorite classes were, it still appears,
my classes in fine art. Yes, they were cool!

We learned to draw and then to shade our drawing;
that objects were not flat we could thus show.
We learned to use our color paints for showing
how objects did appear in sunlight's glow.

It was a special treat when my art teacher
would stop right at my desk to take a peek.
His comments were instructive; their main feature
was that he urged me on when he did speak.

It seems I should have known right from the start
that I should spend my life creating art.

16

Although my mother did appear quite proud
to see a piece of art that I had done,
she never did encourage me out loud
but voiced her view that art was just for fun.

I later learned an uncle that she had,
who was a gifted artist in his time,
was always poor. She deemed it to be sad
that from his art he never earned a dime.

Nor did my father ever encourage me
to be an artist. In his judgment, art
was done by hands, not using brains, you see,
while using brains one should do from the start.

My parents then encouraged me to veer
far from creating art as a career.

17

So I was sent to college to pursue
some serious goals my parents had in mind,
like studying journalism with a view
that I'd report important news I find.

And then to study law they wanted me,
so I could then perhaps have a career
in state or foreign service, as may be,
and help solve crucial problems far or near.

Yes, many years I spent pursuing odd
ideas of how I should spend my time!
If only I had listened to my God
and heard the voice that truly was sublime!

And so your story, Jonah, makes me think
of how between our stories there's a link.

18

Like you I found, O Jonah, no escape
from that eternal God who's our true guide.
He is the one who tries to give some shape
to our lives and does stand by our side.

We may at times attempt to run away
because of ignorance or just from fear,
or sometimes may be simply led astray
by those whom we may hold so very dear,

but in the end we do get on to doing
what our God desires us to do.
There is, I think, no point to then be stewing
over some missed chances and some lost years, too.

I feel so very lucky that one day
I listened to what my God had to say!

ALSO BY THE AUTHOR

INTRODUCTION TO PUBLIC INTERNATIONAL LAW (1955) (Hebrew)
THE BIRD'S LAST SONG (Illustrated by the author) (1976)
HOLOCAUST WALL HANGINGS (2002)
MY LIFE INTO ART: An Autobiography (2007)
LOOKING BACK: Four Plays (2010)
ON BEING AN ARTIST: Three Plays and a Libretto (2012)
REFLECTIONS: Poems, Lyrics, and Stories (With Laura Liberman, M.D.) (2012)
ICE CREAM SNOW (Illustrated by the author) (2012)
PASSION: Poems of Love and Protest (2013)
ZINA: A Selection from Her Poems and Photographs (2013)
THE LITTLE FAIRY (Illustrated by Gail Davis) (2013)
COLOR IN OUR WORLD (Illustrated by the author with photographs) (2014)
THE VERY OLD PAINTER AND HER HUSBAND (Illustrated by Gail Davis) (2014)
HAIFA: My Home Town (Illustrated by Radu Costea) (2014)
ANGEL'S PUPPIES (Illustrated by Gail Davis) (2014)
THE GIANT HOUSE (Illustrated by Gail Davis) (2014)
THE BEE AND THE BUTTERFLY (Illustrated by Radu Costea) (2014)
THE MOUNTAIN (Illustrated by Gail Davis) (2014)
THE TUNNEL (Illustrated by Gail Davis) (2014)
THE OLD DOLL (Illustrated by Gail Davis) (2014)
THE LITTLE SONGBIRD (Illustrated by Gau Family Studio) (2015)
FIFTEEN FABLES (Illustrated by Gail Davis) (2015)
TWELVE MORE FABLES (Illustrated by Gail Davis) (2015)
THE BIRD WHO WENT TO HEAVEN (Illustrated by Gau Family Studio) (2015)
A PARAKEET FOR ERIC (Illustrated by Gail Davis) (2015)
TALES OF HUMAN FOIBLES (Illustrated by Gail Davis) (2015)
THE GIRL AND THE PIGEONS (Illustrated by Gau Family Studio) (2015)
IN THE MILITARY CEMETERY (Illustrated by Gail Davis) (2015)
MORE TALES OF HUMAN FOIBLES (Illustrated by Gail Davis) (2015)
MICHAEL AND THE FLAG (Illustrated by Gail Davis) (2015)
WHAT WILL I BE? (Illustrated by Gau Family Studio) (2016)
IF I HAD THE POWER (Illustrated by Gail Davis) (2016)
IF I WERE RICH (Illustrated by Gail Davis) (2016)
LUCY AND THE SNOWMAN (Illustrated by Gau Family Studio) (2016)
THE WHIRLPOOL (Illustrated by Gail Davis) (2016)
THE LETTERS OF THE ALPHABET (Illustrated by Gail Davis) (2016)
TALE OF THE ROMAN NUMERALS (Illustrated by Gail Davis) (2016)
THE BRIDGE (Illustrated by Gail Davis) (2016)
IF I HAD A LITTLE SISTER (Illustrated by Gau Family Studio) (2016)
GRANDMA'S GLASSES (Illustrated by Gail Davis) (2016)
IF I WERE A MOM (Illustrated by Gau Family Studio) (2016)
THE SECRET (Illustrated by Gau Family Studio) (2016)
ANNE FRANK IN MY ART (Illustrated by the author) (2017)
RUTHIE AND HER ANCESTORS (Illustrated by Al Margolis) (2017)
AN INTRODUCTION TO MY JUDAICA ART (Illustrated by the author) (2017)

(Continued)

(Continued)

RONNIE'S ALARM CLOCK (Illustrated by Gau Family Studio) (2017)
SHOP AND SHOP (Illustrated by Gau Family Studio) (2017)
THE RAINBOW (Illustrated by Gail Davis) (2017)
HEAVENLY GARDENS (Illustrated by Radu Costea) (2017)
HOLOCAUST PAINTINGS (Illustrated by the author) (2017)
HOMO SAPIENS (Illustrated by the author) (2017)
SELF PORTRAITS OF A HOLOCAUST ARTIST (Illustrated by the author) (2017)
YOUR GRANDPA (Illustrated by Gau Family Studio) (2017)
THE TRAIN (Illustrated by Gail Davis) (2017)
MY BIRTHDAY (Illustrated by Gau Family Studio) (2017)
THE WAILING WALL (Illustrated by Gail Davis) (2017)
THE BLANKET (Illustrated by Gail Davis) (2017)
THE FUTURE (Illustrated by Gau Family Studio) (2017)
EXPULSION (Illustrated by Gail Davis) (2017)
QUEEN ESTHER (Illustrated by Gau Family Studio) (2018)
THE SINKING OF THE PATRIA (Illustrated by Gail Davis) (2018)
BEN AND THE BISHOP (Illustrated by Gail Davis) (2018)
THE VISIT TO LATRUN (Illustrated by Gail Davis) (2018)
ROKITNO SQUARE (Illustrated by Gail Davis) (2018)
THE KING (Illustrated by Gau Family Studio) (2018)
MY FRIEND GERARD (Illustrated by Gail Davis) (2018)
GRANDMA'S LESSONS (Illustrated by Gau Family Studio) (2018)
ARON AND HIS GRANDPA (Illustrated by Gail Davis) (2018)
SARAH AND HER GRANDMA (Illustrated by Gail Davis) (2019)
MIRIAM'S DIARY (a novel) (2019)
DAD'S DESK (Illustrated by Gau Family Studio) (2019)
STARTING SCHOOL (Illustrated by Gau Family Studio) (2020)
CHILD'S PLAY: Flash Plays For Children Who Like to Act (2020)
THE SCARECROW AND THE CROW (Illustrated by Gau Family Studio) (2020)
FROM SKETCHES TO PICTURE BOOKS (Illustrated by Gau Family Studio) (2020)
FROM BLACK AND WHITE TO COLOR (Illustrated by Gau Family Studio) (2020)
I WANT A DOG (Illustrated by Al Margolis) (2020)
ROCCO THE GIANT BOY (Illustrated by Al Margolis) (2021)
SONNETS OF LOSS AND TRIUMPH (2021)
SONNETS OF PAIN AND FORGIVENESS (2021)
SELF PORTRAITS (Illustrated by the author) (2021)
CREATING WALL HANGINGS (Illustrated by the author) (2021)
SONNETS OF SETBACK AND HOPE (2021)
SONNETS OF GRIEF AND PRIDE (2021)
SONNETS OF BETRAYAL AND ACCEPTANCE (2021)
SONNETS OF POWER AND HONOR (2021)
SONNETS OF ENVY AND EXILE (2021)

OTHER BOOKS OF SONNETS BY THE AUTHOR

CPSIA information can be obtained
at www.ICGtesting.com
Printed in the USA
BVRC100914031021
617784BV00013B/312